SOMETHING OTHER THAN OTHER

BY THE SAME AUTHOR

together still (Hub Editions, 2004)
where rungs were (Noon Press, 2007)
someone one once ran away with (Longhouse, 2009)
before music (Red Moon Press, 2012)

AS EDITOR

Haiku in English: The First Hundred Years (Norton, 2013; with Jim Kacian & Allan Burns)

SOMETHING OTHER
THAN OTHER

PHILIP ROWLAND

ISOBAR PRESS

Published in 2016 by

Isobar Press
Sakura 2-21-23-202, Setagaya-ku,
Tokyo 156-0053, Japan
&
14 Isokon Flats, Lawn Road,
London NW3 2XD, United Kingdom

http://isobarpress.com

ISBN 978-4-907359-14-0

Copyright © Philip Rowland 2016

All rights reserved.

Contents

I

Prelude	11
In Utero	12
All the Wrong Notes	13
'after / love'	14
'hung between'	15
Vocabulary	16
Snow	17
'snow's'	18
A Few Loose Strands	19
Moonlit	20
'dark / cloud'	21
Prayer	22
Birdsong	23
'absence / of metaphor'	24
Man on a Ladder	25
'dark / i / am / in'	26
Night Shift	27
Distance	28
'just / when'	31
Menashe	32
Buberian	33

II

Surveillance	36

III

Bio Notes	59
Photos of Poets	62
Found in Joseph Ceravolo	64
Found in John Riley	65
Study Notes	66
The Joy of Paradox	68
Seán Rafferty in Conversation	69
'Disillusion: storm'	70
Variation on Ian Hamilton Finlay's 'Acrobats'	71
Hey Dude	72
On Darwin's 200th Birthday	73
'verbatomb'	74

IV

Directives	79
Par	81
'knot in the sunlit floorboard'	82
'anchor'	83
'ringed by horizons'	84
The Moment Lasts Forever	85
'a delay'	86
'breeze a synonym'	87
Down or Across	88
'the pull of grief'	89
'a viola playing'	90
A Bach Fugue	91

Notes & Acknowledgements   93

for Haruka Sophie

I

Prelude

in the hush before music
the music of who
I am not

*

Prelude in C –
winter sky
deep in the piano lid

*

inhabiting repetition
listening for the sound
of our listening

In Utero

strip light flickering
distortion in the amplified
heartbeat

*

wind-blown leaves the fetus dreams a thumbprint

*

pregnant she sleeps
the weight of each released
piano key

*

sealed hotel room window in my dream I suckle a child

*

fatherhood in utero Bach

All the Wrong Notes

a Bach fugue
hands separately
trying to make sense of
the rainy season

*

all the wrong notes granting bones life

*

for whom the gift of my mistakes

after
love

prac
ti

sing
speech

less
ness

hung between
two

absences

like
light waiting

to be let in, to let

us be

Vocabulary

winter closing in …
I visit the simplest words
in the dictionary

*

where my vocabulary clouds clouds

*

this cold morning's
ghost of a meaning
in steam from the tops
of tall buildings

*

deep within
the falling snow
a truer word for it

Snow

words learned in my sleep

an appetite for translation, for what's not, lost in it

poems put into the language of numbers

a line drawn through a misspelled word

debt we have yet to owe

a woman going bald reading a poem

a sensation in dreams, an amorphous membrane one might reach out to touch

approaching a city then walking its streets until dawn

commentary of water upon itself

nothing adding up

getting or not getting the last word

snow's

neither

nor

A Few Loose Strands

the fantasy of a life
without desire –
remaindered moon

*

in a windowless world   seeking osmosis

*

the ocean's
     algorithms …
a few loose strands of hair

Moonlit

who'll go first   moon-viewing

*

goat-bell
  a star
    goes out

*

autumn deepens
the unfathomable
bits of her

*

moonlit
something other
than other

dark
cloud

some
sunlight

sieved
over

darker
sea

Prayer

Not wanting to 'package' this as experience, only to do the wound justice, the wound that's not really mine, or mine only as guilt.

Not to indulge the details, the arbitrariness.

This impulse to prayer – not to a personal God (unthinkable), but as a last gesture, a means of giving form to despair, of giving oneself up utterly and, humbled, finding what's left.

> *whipped by palms a man*
> *swept along by the tsunami*

Birdsong

The dead surround the living. The living are the core of the dead.
    John Berger

To respect the living as the core of the dead.

To aspire in our relation to time to that of the dead to timelessness: to be at rest, tangibly within the medium in which we exist. For life to move towards the condition of music.

The example of Messiaen, who composed his 'Quartet for the End of Time' while interned in a prison camp during World War II. Rehearsed in the lavatory, on broken instruments, the composer later wished to stress the preposition 'for' in the title of the piece – the music directed towards eternity, timelessness.

To praise – aspire – as though transcribing birdsong that the dead might hear.

absence
of metaphor

in air
in the

bones
of birds

Man on a Ladder

after John Davies and Jeffrey Wainwright

wooden man
on a wooden ladder,
his narrow body
contoured and incised
with marks and lines
like language seen
from afar, each limb
on a different rung,
eyes looking neither
up nor down
as if in knowledge
of the nowhere he's
going, a man in
air, out of the air,
out of air

dark
i
am
in

the
dark
i

am
in

the

dark
i

am
in
the

dark
i
am
in

Night Shift

clear winter night –
all the clocks
in the empty classrooms

*

night shift sorting petals returned to sender

*

small hours the squares of night none fits

*

transparent
eyeball
out on a limb

Distance

The Brain – is wider than the Sky –
    Emily Dickinson

Mrs D, a woman of forty, presented the initial complaint of vague but intense fear. She said she was frightened of everything, 'even of the sky'.
    R. D. Laing, *The Divided Self*

But why
'even'? Why not
particularly? After all,
it's hard to think of anything
harder to grasp, more terrifyingly serene
in the distance it keeps between itself and the thing seen,
a word more vertiginous when the structures of meaning are
    collapsing
in on the abyss from which it would otherwise seem
to shield us …

*

everywhere, precariousness,
countless
multitude, terrifying magnitude
of error:

there is no centre, no names
hold, death has
parsed all its sentences
and meets itself everywhere

*

s t a r s f a r s t a r e

the sky
            pulled out from under

*

slippage of self in
time, immeasurable

distance in the head
the head conceives outside

*

out of thin air

and in the thick of it,

whatever we might think,

however thin the seeming thread

just
when
you
think
there's
nothing
there
there's
more
to
nothing
than
you
think

Menashe

the
old

poet's
voice

angelic
his

shoe
lace

less
ness

Buberian

the city's rich calamity
like an embrace

into which I walk
in which I wake

amid the multiplicity
and ordinariness

to the thou
in the stranger's eye

the sheen
upon the skyscrapers

and how the neon
sign against

the early morning winter sky
knows its place

II

Surveillance

for John Levy

under closed circuit
surveillance

old snow

on an island
in the pond

on screens overlooking
the Shinjuku station concourse
seals slithering across a floor

    the   crowd
kissing   the
     of   silence
phones   in
among   every-
    the   thing

night drawing in
a mask in the teeth
of the escalator

        night
     after night
  neon in the river:
the *Hotel Yesterday*

river-shadows lapping bolts beneath the bridge

sunset
where the railway
          bends

Sunday morning
the distant clank of a train
some world or other

mind elsewhere,
          surprised
    by a mannequin

foxed stills outside the porn cinema

early evening
in the stairwell a pimp
pumps a bicycle tire

winter night
the soles of her black high heels
deep red

gladiator

sandals, turquoise

toenails, eye

contact

wind-blown rain
against the crowded train window;
slowly she presses
a fist against it

rush hour a
seeing woman feeling
Braille

an ad for a device that allows one to 'touch truth'

the room within the radius of the blind man's stick

sticky heat at dusk
a boy swings a baseball bat
at calla lilies

in the small hours
the coin laundry's
fish-less tank

dog day afternoon –
the tofu seller's cry ascends
a single tone

first coolness …
　for a moment
　　I see it without a name –
　　　Mt Fuji

in the time it takes the temple bell

an empty hearse
hurries across
the level crossing;

gutter ginkgo
leaf-dust
lifts a little

mourners –
a hole through the roof
for the pine

inside an envelope
inside an envelope
  funeral money

stars
but no moon …
following
steps down
to the crematorium

outside the tomb
inside the stone lantern
a stone

day moon
the plot of earth
between skyscrapers

the dangling ends
of the window washer's ropes

winter
afternoon

sun
striping

one
skyscraper

hiding
another

after Reznikoff

the steel worker still himself upon the girder

road repair crew
gathered round for a briefing
among the roots –
protruding like knuckles –
of a huge, ancient tree

twilight
deepening
the space between the goalposts
painted on a wall

winter dusk
over a deserted construction site
a single wire
ever so slowly
swinging

in chill wind
crows' caws
flapping among
illegible
temple flags

winter sun not wanting to resolve a thing

negotiating the quake
investing in veins
of leaves

radioactive rain …
she speaks of the pain
of divorce

long after the quake the abstract left askew

a square of sun
on a train seat –
my complete in-
complete works

near the edge
of the railway platform
the blind man's feet
perfectly aligned

dapper prof
removes his watch
carefully lays it before
his antipasti

sunshine wrapped in cellophane the suction pads of squid

the chef with shaven eyebrows swiftly slicing clams

winter's bone the smell of sushi

eating alone
forcing a smile
for the selfie

luv at first sight –
her face lit only by the light
of her mobile phone

I CAN'T LIVE WITHOUT YOU.
OK. I WILL SURVIVE.
An oddly low-key resolve
to state publicly, though perhaps
not to have carved with a knife.

rooftop ad
amid
puddled neon:
*I am only doing
what I can do*

bright autumn noon –
a sudden chorus of birds from inside
a briefcase

wing-prints in dust on the terminus girder

mid-afternoon, in the birdshit-spattered
backstreets of Shinjuku, from a room with a view
of beer barrels and bedraggled
bamboo, sense of the homely, unholy
holiness of life resumes

under the elevated railway
a prefab, two-storey
POEM HILLS

autumn leaves a scattering of moles on the monk's bald pate

not a cloud in sight
a cyclist jumps the lights
no-handed

sky *wires* so *wires* blue *wires*

freewheeling
into azure
with a warped front tire

pedestrian crossing
the fractal edge
of cumulonimbus

us and them –
headlights picking out
rain
as we cross

torrential rain
the silence inside
the taxi we share

on the late train home
I am not alone
in talking to myself

III

Bio Notes

puddled night pavement –
the shape my past
refuses to take

*

the unmeant
bent
into life

*

someone masquerading as someone

*

still evening –
at home
in a foreign land
going out of my way
to step in old snow

*

the taste of match
in the first drag –
family revisited

*

leaf I leave
on the floor of
my childhood

*

death
like a foot
tapping the ceiling

*

b. for born d.
for died and

parenthetically
at that

*

morning haze
a student asks what will happen
to my bones

*

measured for a burial:
the distance from
self to word

*

He was trying (they may say)
to say something, but was
too busy chewing on something
mistaken for nothingness.

Photos of Poets

poet so sunk in thought it seems doubtful he'll speak again
poet who has clearly done his thinking and attained an
    unassuming serenity
poet with wife and artist-collaborator in bed
poet skateboarding a Paris pavement
poet making a precise point
poet struggling to keep her hair in place
poet standing dazed in a sunlit glade
poet in a dim light, lit only by his laptop's glare
poet hooded
poet pushing back her hair to reveal an underarm tattoo
poet with her little dog, smiling on behalf of them both
poet hugging a life-size papier-mâché lion
poet with members of the Ladies' Bicycling Association
poet with a ripe apple
poet in profile cut out from newspaper classifieds
poet completely bald, clearly delighted
poet stepping eagerly up to the rostrum
poet presiding over his bone china collection
poet arranging tulips to her incomplete satisfaction
poet looking kindly in Tibetan robes
poet with eyes only showing above his glowing T-shirt
poet pixelated
poet with a finger in each ear, listening intently
poet on the verge of speech
poet with hand on heart and a Panama hat

poet with muscular arms crossed, in front of a slatted fence or
    beach hut
poet browsing through his many large books of visual poetry
poet holding a disposable camera at arm's length, photograph-
    ing himself
poet with lips pursed, in mid-decision
poet in defiantly heavy lipstick
poet nibbling his girlfriend's ear
poet perched on a rock beneath a mountain pine
poet hunched attentively forward
poet with long hair and prophetic beard who's just been
    listening to the Chico Hamilton Quintet
poet in conversation with another poet in a bare corner of an
    art gallery
poet in top hat, holding a rubber toy replica of Godzilla
poet in a snappy snakeskin suit, perched on the edge of a 70's
    hotel room bed
poet at an antique desk in a see-through fluffy dress, nibbling
    her pen-tip
poet giving his best man's speech
poet at dawn on the beach
poet giving a grizzled, disarmingly direct stare
poet gazing out to sea
poet awash in books, leaning back in his chair
poet teaching cross-legged on a desk
poet who refuses, on principle, to supply a photo
poet carefully lifting the lid of a piano

Found in Joseph Ceravolo

What landscape should I stalk
all alone
happy as a stone?

The forecast is a dusting
of perfumes
rising in the flood

Like a punch in the face
the look of the end
a windless chase

The fishes lie in place
I enter into the exultation
dogs know

Lice in heaven.
Inoculated sheep
like words, words, words

Found in John Riley

the scent of bluebells
CZARGRAD
iron in the blood

sharing their breath
Russians walk in
the very soft breezes

to attend to objects
flick away the one
fluttering down

resurrection of the trees
fury of stars
on a cloudless night

dream formalism
But is his chute open?
this face-saving sop

Study Notes

i.

mediocre   mediocre
preliminary   marginal
superfluous   superfluous
futile   futile   futile   filthy   filthy
filthy   filthy   vulgar

or so she has written
in her English notebook

ii.

scrawled angst
etched anxiety
imprint of despair

iii.

mind
ful
minus

iv.

shall I compare thee
shall I compare the
shall I compare th
shall I compare t
shall I compare
shall I compar
shall I compa
shall I comp
shall I com
shall I co
shall I c
shall I
shall
shal
sha
sh

v.

meaning is like happiness
how the verge turns out
to be the real thing

The Joy of Paradox

one keeps running away with
someone one
once ran away with

Seán Rafferty in Conversation

I like vegetables,
you can eat them and
they don't talk to you.

Disillusion: storm
　in a teacup
　in a storm

Variation on Ian Hamilton Finlay's 'Acrobats'

```
b       b       b       b       b
    a       a       a       a
s       s       s       s       s
        t       t       t       t
a       a       a       a       a
    r       r       r       r
d       d       d       d       d
        s       s       s       s
d       d       d       d       d
    r       r       r       r
a       a       a       a       a
        t       t       t       t
s       s       s       s       s
    a       a       a       a
b       b       b       b       b
```

Hey Dude

hey dude do you understand
that there is aliens that are

demons ok . Dont any
1 get it that these ships are

real . im telling you
i know . see

the problem is everybody
belives by the book

of the bible of what it sez
open your mind man .

On Darwin's 200ᵗʰ Birthday

wedged (as Darwin
said) against

death as if
under the weight

of the nothing
everything

amounts to
on premises

long since
evacuated

verbatomb

IV

Directives

i.

to speak
holding the silence

at the back of your mouth
like an unuttered greeting

ii.

after Oppen

to find just
the right weight
up against the fact
of what the poem
didn't create

iii.

to stay within
the current
of continual
arrival –

to know where
to turn when
sense dis-
solves back

into the quotidian
leaving the gift
a mere
quota

iv.
      Levinas Meets Lawrence

the ruination of the step
in the performance of the step itself

as, with each poem, we
bruise an exit from ourselves?

Par

for the course:
in via

the trap door

out
the vent

knot in the sunlit floorboard undone by prayer

anchor
i
tic

ringed by horizons
of yesterdays –
quick to mistake a sail

The Moment Lasts Forever

for Burton Watson

for all these storms and streams no north of the present

*

index of moments i'm neither here nor there

*

fleeing the
moment lasts
forever

a delay in large leaves

breeze a synonym for ash

Down or Across

my last visit there was
nothing to say, nothing for us

to do but the crossword:
to find comfort in clues

to words with
nothing to do

with her terminal predicament,
nothing to do but go

down or across
gradually accumulating

final sense
with nothing to do

with the ward

the pull of grief
at dawn
through drawn curtains
the oddly musical
whine of machinery

a viola playing
a piece for cello –
autumn deeper

*

snowflakes thickening
a harpsichord's twang
in the bass

A Bach Fugue

the bare tree brimming
winter morning sunlight –

the notes just
notes, marks on a page

*

dusk   rearranging silences

*

what's left of the light the music absorbs

Notes & Acknowledgements

A FEW LOOSE STRANDS The second part of this piece borrows a phrase from a haiku by Jim McKay: 'staring at the Buddhists / on the F train / seeking osmosis'.

DISTANCE The third part of this piece borrows from Laura Riding's poem 'The Map of Places' ('Death meets itself everywhere') while the fifth part quotes from her 'Opening of Eyes' ('And thus do false horizons claim pride / For distance in the head / The head conceives outside').

§

Many thanks to Isobar publisher and editor Paul Rossiter for his close collaboration and valuable suggestions at all stages of the preparation of this book.

Thanks also to the editors of the following journals, where many of these poems (or versions of these poems) were first published: *Acorn, American Tanka, Big Bridge, Blithe Spirit, Bongos of the Lord,* CLWN WR, *Ekleksographia, Frogpond, The Heron's Nest, Hummingbird, is/let,* MASKS, *Modern Haiku, Origin* (Sixth Series), *Otata, Pinstripe Fedora, Presence, Roadrunner, Salamander Cove, South by Southeast,* and *still: a journal of short verse.*

A number of the poems have appeared in the following books and anthologies: *The Blue Planet* (Hokumeisha, 2011), *Fire in the Treetops* (Press Here, 2015), *Haiku in English: The First Hundred Years* (Norton, 2013), *Haiku 21* (Modern Haiku Press, 2011), *Salutations: A Festschrift for Burton*

Watson (Ahadada/Ekleksographia, 2015), and *Stepping Stones: A Way into Haiku* (British Haiku Society, 2007); others appeared in Red Moon Press annual anthologies of English-language haiku: *Carving Darkness* (2011), *Fear of Dancing* (2013), and *Galaxy of Dust* (2015).

Several of the poems first appeared in the chapbooks *someone one once ran away with* (Longhouse, 2009) and *where rungs were* (Noon Press, 2007). A selection of haiku from *before music* (Red Moon Press, 2012) are re-presented here in new configurations and in some cases revised form.

www.ingramcontent.com/pod-product-compliance
Lightning Source LLC
Chambersburg PA
CBHW031205090426
42736CB00009B/789